YOU CHOOSE
BOOKS

THE HAUNTED SANATORIUM

A CHILLING INTERACTIVE ADVENTURE

by Matt Doeden
and Mari Bolte

CAPSTONE PRESS
a capstone imprint

You Choose Books are published by Capstone Press,
1710 Roe Crest Drive, North Mankato, Minnesota 56003
www.mycapstone.com

Library of Congress Cataloging-in-Publication Data
Cataloging-in-Publication Data is available on the Library of Congress website.
ISBN 978-1-5157-3651-6 (library binding)
ISBN 978-1-5157-3656-1 (ebook pdf)

Editorial Credits
Heidi Thompson, designer; Wanda Winch, media researcher;
Gene Bentdahl, production specialist

Photo Credits
Delcampe Auctions: scview, 66; Ebay: Double C Antiques, 13; Institute for Regional Studies, NDSU, Fargo (200.437.13), 76; Library of Congress: Prints and Photographs Division, 61; Shutterstock: Anders E. Skanberg, 42, boscorelli, cover (top), 1, Daniel Schmitt, cover (bottom), 30, Fotokon, 32, Grischa Georgiew, 57, happykanppy, watercolor background, Igor Vitkovskiy, fog design, Inked Pixels, 23, John Arehart, 4, Kotsovolos Panagiotis, 54, Mariusz Niedzwiedzki, 71, momente, 39, phildaint, 93, Plateresca, torn paper design, Puwadol Jaturawutthichai, 88, Roman Nerud, 85, run4it, grunge paper texture, saki80, grunge frame, SanchaiRat, 9, Stefan Schierle, 6, 16, 18, 36, 46, 68, STILLFX, grey grunge texture, Valentidaze, 98

Printed in Canada.
10050S17

TABLE OF CONTENTS

INTRODUCTION

YOU are about to enter the run-down remains of a long-abandoned sanatorium. Decades ago, it was a hospital for those stricken with a terrible disease called tuberculosis—also known as consumption, the White Plague, and the White Death.

Now, in this shell of a hospital, only the ghosts of the past remain—but could that be more than just an expression here? Do you run? Hide? Or do you confront the supernatural forces at work and try to learn the deep secrets of this haunted relic? Your choices will guide the story. Turn the page and follow the directions to find out what happens next.

Many sanatoriums were built in the late 1800s and early 1900s to treat tuberculosis patients.

THE SPACE
FOR THE SICK

The sun hangs low in the sky, just peeking out over the treetops. It casts long shadows onto the massive building that looms dead ahead. You stand with your two best friends, Luisa and Mitch, staring up at five stories of concrete and broken glass. You were dared by some kids at school to spend the night here. It seemed simple to accept the challenge. Now, you're having second thoughts.

The Haunted Sanatorium. For years you've heard local rumors and urban legends about this abandoned hospital. The forest surrounding the hospital, chosen long ago for the fresh air and quiet atmosphere for patients, now seems dark and ominous.

Turn the page.

You shake your head. You haven't even stepped inside, but already your imagination is running away with you! But then a small movement in the windows high above catches your eye—a scurrying shadow. You shudder with the feeling that you're being watched.

I'm imagining things, you think. *It's just a building.*

"Are we sure we want to do this?" Luisa asks.

"We'll never hear the end of it if we don't," answers Mitch.

He's right. The three of you took a dare. In your circle of friends, there's no backing out. "Come on, guys," you say, managing to sound more confident than you really feel. "All the stories, they're just stories. It's a camping trip. But instead of being in a tent, we'll be ... you know ... in there."

Resolved, you step forward, backpack slung over one shoulder and sleeping bag over the other. The front door is locked, but there are no shortage of windows to crawl through. In a matter of seconds, you're inside, quietly padding down a long-abandoned hallway.

The building feels cold. A draft wafts through the hall. The sound of your footsteps echoes off the concrete walls, which are stripped of paint and covered in graffiti.

Hundreds of thousands of Americans died each year from tuberculosis in the early 1900s.

Turn the page.

"Check this out," Mitch says, pointing to some of the painted designs. The three of you stop to look. A dark, vaguely human-shaped shadow created in spray paint crawls across the wall. It's so realistic that it gives you shivers. "I think it's supposed to be some sort of ghost," Mitch says. "I ..."

Mitch stops mid-sentence, his mouth hanging open. It takes a moment for you to realize what he already knows. The three of you are standing still. But the sound of footsteps is still in the air.

Then they stop. The laughter begins. It's a cold and hollow sound. It resonates through the corridor, as if mocking you.

To investigate, go to page 11.

To search for a place to hide, turn to page 14.

"What do you think that was?" you ask, squinting as you stare down the hallway. For a moment, you were scared. Now, you're just curious. You really want to know who—or what—made that sound. Your friends begin to protest, but you run directly toward the direction of the laughter.

Everything happens in an instant. You slam into something and sprawl to the ground. The thing—person?—you ran into grunts as it hits the floor too.

"Relax!" says a familiar voice. You sit up, rubbing your head in confusion.

"Ethan?" you groan. "What are you doing here?" Mitch's older brother gives a little wave, then winces, massaging his shoulder.

Turn the page.

You grin. Knowing he took the worst of the impact helps take some of the sting out of your own wound.

"Were you scared?" Ethan taunts. "Mitch told me you guys were coming, and I couldn't resist. I just wanted to mess with you a bit." He gives you a playful slap on the back.

"Go home, Ethan," Mitch growls. "We don't want you here."

Ethan shoots you one last grin. "Don't let the g-g-g-ghosts get ya!" he says, then disappears down the hallway, chuckling all the way.

"Well, now we've seen our first restless spirit," Luisa jokes, brushing dirt off your back. "Things should be a piece of cake from here on out. Where to next?"

Luisa wants to check out the Water Room, supposedly one of the most haunted rooms in the sanatorium. Mitch suggests finding a spot to set up camp for the night. They turn to you. What will you choose?

To start preparing a spot to camp, turn to page 18.

To head to the Water Room, turn to page 32.

Experts believe around 1,600 tuberculosis patients died at Tranquille Sanatorium in Kamloops, British Columbia. Today it is known as one of the most haunted places in Canada.

Your heart races. "Let's get out of here," you whisper. Your friends don't need much convincing. The three of you turn and rush down the hallway, all but bouncing off the walls in your hurry to get away from ... whatever that was.

"Come on!" Luisa cries. She dives into a room, dragging you behind her. You whirl and slam the door shut, then stand with your backs to the wall in silence. You even try to breathe quietly.

The sound of slow footsteps starts out as a whisper. But they draw closer and closer. The hairs on the back of your neck stand up with each step. Your hands are shaking.

The footsteps stop outside the closed door. You hold your breath as the door slowly opens, squeaking on its rusty hinges. You back into a corner as far you can. Will you run or try to be tough? Even now you don't know.

"BOO!" A figure charges in through the door. Mitch screams. You're about to do the same when you realize that the figure is bent over, laughing. It's just Mitch's older brother, Ethan!

"Oh man, you should have seen your faces!" he taunts. "When Mitch said you were coming here, and all alone, it was just too good an opportunity to pass up."

Mitch is fuming. He steps up and slugs Ethan in the shoulder.

"You're a jerk," he says.

"You're the one who screamed like a baby," Ethan taunts. He mimics a baby's cry.

Mitch's face falls, and Ethan seems to realize he's gone too far. "Come on, little bro. Let's get you home," he says. "I won't tell anyone about this, and I know your friends won't either."

Turn the page.

15

Mitch nods, then looks up sheepishly. "Sorry guys," he says. "I'm going with Ethan."

You try to talk him out of leaving. "No, come on, Mitch. Stay." But it's pointless. You can tell that he's made up his mind.

"I'm going too," Luisa says. "This seemed like a good idea before. Now … what are we even doing here? I just want to go home."

Today many sanatoriums across the United States stand empty.

"What?" You stand there, dumbfounded. "We've been here five minutes. Give it a shot, come on."

But you can't talk them out of it. "Sorry," Luisa says. "Are you coming?"

To remain here and spend the night alone, turn to page 21.

To leave the haunted sanatorium with your friends, turn to page 51.

You agree with Mitch. If you're staying the night, there will be plenty of time to explore. You'd rather get yourselves set up for the night. The three of you wander through the first floor, debating where to make camp. The old building is full of crumbling debris and garbage, so there aren't as many options as you had hoped.

Abandoned sanatoriums, asylums, and hospitals are often looted or vandalized by trespassers.

You circle back to the main entrance. It juts out from the rest of the building, supported by heavy pillars. "This seems like as good a spot as any," says Mitch timidly. "We're technically inside the building. But, you know, it's easy to get out if things get … weird."

"Pfff," Luisa scoffs. "Are you kidding me?" She stops for a moment, setting down her bag to dig through the pockets.

"What are you looking for?" you ask, annoyed at her delay. The longer you debate, the less time you'll have to explore.

"I've got a map of this place right here," Luisa says proudly, pulling it out of her bag. "And you know what's right around the corner?"

"What?" Mitch asks, interested.

Turn the page.

Luisa jabs at the map. "It's the electroshock therapy room, where they used to treat people by shocking them with huge doses of electricity. *That's* where we should set up camp."

Both heads turn toward you. "Come on, tiebreaker," Luisa says. "What's it going to be?"

To make camp at the main entrance, turn to page 27.

To find the electroshock therapy room, turn to page 29.

"Aw, come on," you call out, watching your friends leave. "Stay, it's going to be a fun night!"

Neither of them even bothers to look back.

"Fine," you mutter to yourself. "I'll show them. I'm not scared."

You stand up straight, ignoring the queasy feeling in the pit of your stomach, and start to explore. Several attempts have been made to renovate the old building, but it stands largely in ruin now. Cracked concrete walls and floors, broken windows, and areas where garbage has piled up are everywhere.

Every now and then, a gust of wind whistles through the place with a ghostly wail. It gives you goosebumps, but in a good way. After all, you know ghosts aren't real. But the chill makes your imagination run wild and your adventure seem more fun.

Turn the page.

You make your way up to the third floor. At the top of the steps, a woman stands, waiting. She's wearing a white dress and an old-fashioned nurse's bonnet. Something about her doesn't seem right. When you look closely, you realize that you can see through her.

"You seem to be short of breath," she says. "Has the consumption set in again?"

"Wh-what?" you stammer. "No, I'm just a little winded … the stairs, there are a lot of them …"

"Come with me," the nurse says, reaching out a hand.

To go with the nurse, go to page 23.

To refuse the ghost's request, turn to page 25.

"Uh, OK," you say, reaching out to take the nurse's hand. To your surprise, she feels solid, if very, very cold. She leads you into a small office-like space.

"Now, before we can start your care, you need to sign this form," she says, placing a piece of paper in front of you.

"What … what is this?" you ask. The paper appears to be supernatural too. You can't seem to make out any of the writing.

Patient rooms line the hallways of this sanatorium.

Turn the page.

"Just a simple form," she answers. "Acknowledgement that death may occur, permission to perform an autopsy if you do meet an untimely end, agreement to our hospital's rules, that sort of thing. All right then!" She whisks the paper away before you can sign. "Let's be on our way!"

"But I didn't agree to anything," you protest.

The nurse doesn't seem to hear you. She takes hold of your hand again, and no amount of struggling can loosen her grip.

To keep struggling, turn to page 53.

To distract the nurse and run, turn to page 60.

"No," you say. "No, I'm feeling fine, thanks!"

The nurse reaches for you. You turn and flee, taking the steps a half dozen at a time. You don't know if you're being followed, but you can't take the risk to check. You keep going down until you realize that you've gone down one flight too many. Instead of coming out near the lobby, you find yourself in the basement. Straight ahead is a doorway, and through the doorway you can see a dark hole.

That must be the body chute that they used to move dead bodies, you think. *Too bad Luisa's not here.* You touch your phone in your pocket. It would just take a second to snap a picture for your friend. You imagine how jealous she would be, and you grin. It's tempting.

Turn the page.

As you stand there trying to decide what to do next, you suddenly feel the temperature drop. You turn. A pale blue shape takes form behind you. It's a patient—a young girl. She's holding her hands over her eyes and trembling with pain. "Please, help!" she pleads. "My name ... my name is Ruth. I'm a patient here, and ..." She drops her hands and shrieks, "MY EYES! THEY'VE TAKEN MY EYES!"

You freeze. Now you really have to make a decision. Will you run through Ruth and back up the stairs toward the main exit, or try to escape through the body chute?

To run for the main exit, turn to page 63.

To try to escape through the body chute, turn to page 65.

"The entrance seems like the perfect spot," you say. Mitch is right. It's the best of both worlds. You start unrolling your sleeping bag as Luisa begins to tell a ghost story. Before long, the three of you are trading spooky tales, with only a single flashlight beam keeping you out of complete darkness. Luisa tells a whopper about the Water Room, complete with an evil nurse, tiny little ghostly goblins, and a terrifying and angry spirit.

Just as Luisa's story gets to its scariest part, a huge *THUMP* echoes through the building. All three of you scream.

"What was that?" Luisa asks. Neither of you have an answer. *THUMP!* "There it is again!"

The noise seems to be coming from one floor above you.

Turn the page.

"M—m—maybe it's just the wind," Mitch stammers nervously.

"Maybe it's a ghost!" Luisa says brightly. "Either of you two want to check it out?"

You can tell that Mitch would rather stay put. You're not sure what you want. You're having so much fun just hanging out here, telling ghost stories. But then, wouldn't a real ghost hunt be even more fun?

To investigate, turn to page 47.

To stay put and ignore the sound, turn to page 79.

You shrug your shoulders and give Mitch a look of apology. "We're here, so let's do it right. Sleeping at the front door doesn't seem like much of an adventure."

And so you follow Luisa to the electroshock therapy room. The room's heavy door creaks as you push it open. You step inside, half expecting to be able to feel the electricity in the air. But it just feels like any other room. A bit cold, a bit musty.

"Dibs on that!" Luisa cries, pointing to the corner. There sits a long, narrow table, set beneath a small window. "That's my bed tonight!"

Mitch groans. "You're twisted, Luisa. You know that's probably where they shocked the patients."

Turn the page.

Electroshock therapy (known as electroconvulsive therapy today) is still a technique used by doctors to treat depression. However, in the wrong hands it could be misused on unruly patients.

While they argue the merits of shock therapy, you step up to the table. You place your fingers on its surface, again half expecting to feel the current. But it is cold and lifeless. Disappointed, and bored with your friends' debate, you boost yourself onto the table.

What was that? You flinch. Whatever it was, it felt like a tingle, a tiny spark. It was faint. So faint, you're almost sure you must have imagined it. But then, you feel it again. You place your hands on the table, feeling the cool surface.

Lie down. A voice … a whisper, so quiet it sounds like it comes from inside your head. *Lie down.*

Luisa and Mitch seem oblivious to whatever is happening to you here. You fear for your sanity, yet you feel a powerful urge to lie down, to see what will happen. Then again, maybe listening to voices—even voices in your head—isn't the best idea.

To lie down on the table, turn to page 35.

To stand up and tell your friends what just happened, turn to page 38.

You and Luisa leave Mitch behind to set up. "The Water Room was where doctors treated sick patients with hydrotherapy," Luisa says as you step through the doorway.

You shiver. The room seems to be colder than the rest of the building. You can almost see your breath. You can't imagine what it must have been like to be a patient here. "Hydro-*what?*" you ask, rubbing your arms for warmth.

Hydrotherapy was thought to be good for both the body and the mind. It is still used today. But, like electroshock therapy, it could be abused.

"Hydrotherapy," Luisa says idly, examining what looks like an old hose hanging off the wall. "Patients could be wrapped in wet blankets for hours, or sprayed with really hot or really cold water, or strapped into bathtubs of steaming water for days at a time. They thought it would help cure them." You make eye contact. "Of course, it didn't work," she says.

"This place is creepy," Mitch says, coming up behind you. "I picked somewhere a *lot* less weird to camp, by the way."

"Check this out," Luisa says from a dark corner. "There's an isolation tank back here."

"What's that?" you ask.

"A huge bathtub," Luisa explains. "They'd fill them with warm salt water and shut you in. It was supposed to be relaxing."

Turn the page.

"Dare you to get in," Mitch says, winking.

You stare into the deep tub. It's like an old-fashioned claw-foot tub, only bigger and taller. *Definitely large enough to fit a body*, you think, and then cringe. The top is covered with a ragged bit of fabric. It's kind of icky, but—you tell yourself—not really that scary.

"Well," says Mitch. "You going in or not?"

To get in the tub, turn to page 41.

To leave, turn to page 44.

Your head suddenly feels heavy, and some unseen force compels you to swing your feet up on the table and lie back.

Then it all happens in an instant. A blinding light flashes and the room spins. As your eyes refocus, you realize that everything has changed. The room is the same, yet different. The walls are no longer cracked and chipped. Lights shine down from above. The air is dry and smells faintly of bleach. You hear the sounds of people moving through the hallways. Everything seems to be happening in a haze. Is this a dream?

As you try to sit up, pain flashes through your chest. You try to suck in a breath, but it feels as if your lungs have been filled with cement. You wheeze and gasp, desperate to pull in air. It's like invisible hands are choking you, fingers wrapping around your throat.

Turn the page.

You fall back, your body racked with a fit of coughing. Instinctively, you cover your cough with your hand. When you pull your hand away, it's flecked with blood and mucus.

The room spins. You feel a strange sense of detachment. In that moment, you feel lost. You're not sure you even remember your name.

Beelitz Sanatorium in Germany was built in 1898. It was completely abandoned in 1994.

As every second passes, this new world seems more and more real. A woman enters the room—a nurse. A memory flashes through your mind—a memory of this place, but in ruins.

You shake your head, trying to wrap your mind around it. It's gone as quickly as it arrived, though. The more you try to remember, the more your chest hurts. After a moment, the memory is completely gone.

The nurse leans over you. "Shall we begin with the therapy?" she asks.

To say yes, turn to page 85.

To say no, turn to page 88.

"You guys won't believe this," you say, interrupting Mitch and Luisa's argument. You explain to them what you felt and heard. For a long moment, the two of them just stare at you. Then, together, they burst into a fit of laughter.

"Save the spooky stories for later," Luisa says, punching you playfully on the shoulder. You start to protest, but then decide against it. It does sound crazy. Yet, as the three of you set down your sleeping bags, you're careful to set yours as far from the table as possible.

Once your bags are in place, you decide it's time to do a little exploring. Now that night has fully fallen, the building seems somehow older—and bigger. The sounds of your footsteps in the corridors seem very small compared to the scale of the place.

"Check it out," says Luisa. She points to a sign that reads MORGUE. "Let's go see what's in there."

"I've heard tons of stories about people hearing voices in the morgue," you say, excited. "Do you think we'll see a ghost?"

"One can only hope!" Luisa exclaims.

Some sanatoriums had their own morgue. Others relied on undertakers and funeral home employees to collect deceased patients.

Turn the page.

You can tell that Mitch is just about to protest when ... *THUMP!* Something seems to shake the very foundation of the building. All three of you freeze in your tracks. "What was that?" you whisper. A few seconds pass in silence. You just start to let your guard down when ... *THUMP!* There it is again!

"It seems to be coming from upstairs," Mitch says. He's right. It sounds like some huge weight is being tossed around right above you.

"Could it be your brother playing another prank on us?" you ask.

Mitch shakes his head. "I don't think so. He doesn't have the patience to wait that long."

To investigate the noise, turn to page 47.

To continue on to the morgue, turn to page 91.

With a deep breath, you nod your head. "Yeah. I'm going in."

Your palms are suddenly sweaty. You take an extra grip on your flashlight. You have to will your legs to obey, but they finally step high enough to clear the lip of the tub. Shaking slightly, you lie back.

The fabric over the tub suddenly sweeps over you. The top of the tub is covered, leaving you in the dark. The only light you can see is from the small head hole.

"You guys!" you shout, punching at the fabric. Terror, anger, and panic are all you can feel. "This isn't funny!"

"We're not doing it!" Luisa's muffled voice insists. For a moment, you see a flash of her face through the hole in the fabric. "We're trying to get it off, but it's on here tight!"

Turn the page.

You can hear scratching on the side of the tub, and you see glimpses of light as their flashlights flail back and forth. But otherwise, it's pitch black. Your heart rate rises as you start to panic.

The gentle sound of running water soothes you slightly. Suddenly you realize your feet, and then your entire backside, are wet. The air becomes thick with steam, and you can taste salt in the air droplets that collect on your face.

Hydrotherapy was—and still is—used in asylums, sanatoriums, and prisons around the world. Even Alcatraz Prison had a hydrotherapy room.

At first, you try to get free, splashing and kicking. But you tire quickly, and the warm, salty water sloshing back and forth relaxes your muscles. Soon your body stops responding to your brain. Your eyes begin to close. The sounds of your friends' voices begin to fade.

To keep struggling, turn to page 71.

To stay where you are, turn to page 73.

You're not usually one to turn down a good dare. But there's no way you're getting in that dirty old tub—especially now that you know a little more about hydrotherapy. The tub is so shadowed in the back of the room that you can't even see the bottom. To you, it looks like a pit into nowhere. "Maybe another time," you say, taking a small step back.

Luisa swats you playfully on the shoulder. "You're the last person I'd expect to get spooked by a bathtub," she teases. "Come on, let's see what's next door."

Before you can say a word, Luisa heads out of the Water Room and into the hallway. You leave in time to see her stride confidently into the next room. You feel an odd instinct to reach out and grab her, but she disappears into the darkness before you can move.

Then—the door slams shut! Luisa screams from inside. You and Mitch rush to her aid, but no matter how hard you push or pull, the door doesn't budge. You rattle the door, feeling useless as Luisa screams, before going completely silent.

"Bash the door down," Mitch suggests. The door is old and doesn't look very solid. You both take a few steps back. Then, on the count of three, you charge, throwing your shoulders into the door. The rotten wooden frame splinters as you crash your full weight into it. You and Mitch go tumbling head over heels into the room.

What you see inside is unlike anything you've ever experienced before.

The walls are bathed in a cool blue glow. Luisa lies on the floor, unconscious. You can see your friend clearly, though, and she's definitely breathing. But that's not what causes your panic.

Turn the page.

45

A ghostly nurse hangs above her, anger rolling off her in a supernatural mist. You fear for your friend's life.

To try to rescue Luisa and run, turn to page 74.

To attack the ghost, turn to page 76.

To flee, turn to page 95.

Many sanatoriums are rumored to be haunted by the many patients who passed away in them.

You're ready for a ghostly adventure. "Let's go check it out!" you say, giving Luisa a big grin. She's up and on her feet in a heartbeat. You pretend not to notice that it takes Mitch a bit longer. He's reluctant, but he doesn't protest.

Luisa leads the way to the second floor. As you reach the top step, you hear what can only be described as a bump in the night.

You look around. You can't see anything strange. But then—there it is again. *THUMP!* And it's much louder now.

You have to find out where the sound is coming from. Cautiously, the three of you move down the corridor. Your steps kick up dust, making mesmerizing swirls in the beams of your flashlights.

Turn the page.

A sudden, cold sensation drifts over your skin, making you shiver. You don't think anything could make you more nervous than you are now. Then, there it is again—*THUMP!* The sound is right behind you, causing you to spin so quickly you lose your balance.

"Watch it!" Mitch says, steadying you.

"Over here," Luisa calls. "I've found what's making the noise."

It's a door. You watch as it eases itself open, then slams shut with a loud *THUMP!* You tap the door open with a gentle push of your fingers. From inside the room, a gust of wind from a broken window whips around your face.

"Ha!" Mitch says, relief clear in his tone. "It's just the wind. Don't you feel stupid now? Because I sure do ..."

You let out your breath, realizing that you'd been holding it all that time. You and Mitch both start to laugh.

You turn to Luisa, expecting her to be laughing too. But one look at her face brings you down again. She's staring right into the patient room, a terrified expression on her face.

"What's that?" she whispers, pointing a shaking finger into the corner of the room.

It takes you a moment to spot what she sees, but there, on the far side of the room, lurks a dark, shadowy spot. It's vaguely human in shape. It has to be one of your own shadows, right? But you wave your arm and the shadow doesn't move. You squint your eyes and take a small step forward. Is it just a trick of the light?

Turn the page.

Then the shadow moves, as if awakened by your presence. It may be human in shape, but something about the way it moves—jerky and fluid all at the same time—makes you think of a spider. It seems to surge out of the corner, clinging to the wall as though gravity doesn't matter. You scream.

Mitch's voice rings out, "RUN!"

You charge out of the door, practically tripping over Luisa in your panic. Just down the hall—only a few dozen feet away—hangs a sign that reads FIRE ESCAPE. The other way leads toward the stairwell you took up here in the first place.

To dash for the fire escape, turn to page 81.

To head back toward the stairs, turn to page 83.

Staying the night in a haunted hospital with friends is one thing. Staying the night all by yourself is quite another. What if something happens? Who would know?

Looking around at this big, empty ruin of a building, you decide that's one adventure you don't care to have—at least, not by yourself. The building will always be here to explore if you ever want to try again. So you shrug your shoulders and head out with your friends.

Mitch still looks downcast. You put an arm around him on the way out. "Don't worry about it, buddy," you tell him. "Nobody sane would have stayed there, fake ghosts or not."

He gives you a little smile. "It wasn't just Ethan," he says. "I swear. Something inside the building ... I just didn't think that was somewhere we should be tonight."

Turn the page.

The four of you step outside into twilight, leaving the building—and its secrets—behind you for good. The sun has dipped below the trees now, and everything seems twice as spooky. Maybe it's for the best that you're leaving. You turn for one final look at the building. As you do, a flash of something dark catches your eye.

A whisper, something faint, seems to roll off the shadows. "Don't come back," it hisses.

You won't. You definitely won't.

THE END

To follow another path, turn to page 10.
To learn more about tuberculosis and sanatoriums,
turn to page 99.

You keep struggling. But no matter what you do, the nurse's grip never loosens. She drags you through hallways that never seem to end. You quickly lose your sense of direction.

The crumbling, graffiti-covered walls seem to transform before your eyes, becoming clean and new again. Broken windows repair themselves. And you begin to see ghostly patients appear.

The nurse throws you into a room at the end of a hallway. The door shuts behind you before you can react. Rubbing your wrist, you notice the ghost left a white, skeletal handprint on your skin. You shiver and look around the room.

There are four beds here. Three ghostly children, a girl and two boys, sit huddled on the nearest bed. One, a young girl, beckons to you. You shrug and sit next to her. She says something, but you can't understand.

Turn the page.

53

"What?" you ask.

"Sorry," she says quietly. "I'm only allowed to whisper."

"It's our resting time," one boy explains.

"Soon we'll be resting forever," the other murmurs grimly.

"We're not supposed to talk about it," the girl whispers harshly. She begins to cough.

The sanatorium on Mount Parnitha in Greece, was built in 1912. Many of Athens' sick were treated for tuberculosis there.

"What aren't you supposed to talk about?" you ask. The ghostly children don't seem to be doing very well. You wish you had a blanket to cover them.

"Not getting better," the second boy says. "But they put us in one of the end rooms. They put the sickest patients here. They're next to the elevators, so when we die they can move our bodies to the basement—and then out of the sanatorium—without other patients seeing."

"I just want to see the sun one more time," the first boy says. He starts to cry.

To escape alone and head for the basement, turn to page 56.

To help the children get to the sanatorium's roof, turn to page 68.

"I'm sorry," you say, backing away. "I can't help." You throw yourself at the door, desperate to get out. To your surprise, it's not locked. As you turn to shut the door, the ghost childrens' sad faces are the last thing you see.

You jab the DOWN button for the elevator until the doors open. You jump on and press the button for the basement. *There has to be a way out through the basement,* you think.

The doors ding and you step out onto the bottom floor. Everything is dark and seems to have reverted back to the abandoned old building you first entered. You click on your flashlight and sweep it across the room. There's a doorway! You rush over to open it. When you hold your flashlight up again, what you see takes your breath away.

Future Nazi leader Adolph Hitler was treated at the sanatorium in Beelitz, Germany, during World War I (1914–1918), earning it the nickname "Hitler's Hospital."

You're looking down a long, dark tunnel. Heavy, unfinished walls press in from every side. You can almost feel the massive weight of the building above you. It's like stepping into a nightmare. But there's no going back now.

Your footsteps echo off of the walls, making the tunnel seem even more narrow. Crawl spaces lead toward vast networks of pipes. Just looking at them gives you a wave of claustrophobia.

Turn the page.

The air seems to vibrate as there's a loud *SLAM!* behind you. You whirl around only to see a figure materialize in the air just feet from your face. It's an old woman, her face twisted in pain and rage. A blue glow seems to radiate off of her.

"Ruth has been here for a long time," she hisses. "Are you the one who left Ruth here?"

"N-n-no," you stammer, backing away.

"Ruth is tired of being lied to," she says. "Ruth is tired of being a prisoner." A blast of cold air hits you as she swoops forward. You can see your scared reflection in her black eyes. "Perhaps it is your turn to be Ruth's prisoner!"

The beam of your flashlight swings wildly back and forth as you sprint away from her. But no matter how fast you run, Ruth is faster.

You come to an open doorway and, without a second thought, dart inside. Long metal tables line the walls. Beyond is a large opening in the wall. This must be the chute hospital workers used to use to dispose of dead patients. If local legends are right, the tunnel leads several hundred feet down to some railroad tracks.

You can hear Ruth's wails growing closer.

Turn to page 65.

"Wait!" you yell. "There's a patient over there! He—he's having some sort of attack!" You wave wildly but at nothing specific. The ghost nurse stops, looks around, and then drops your arm to rush into a nearby room. You're free!

But where will you go? You dash for the main exit. But when you burst through the doors, the sun shines bright in your face. The building is new, with fresh paint, clear windows, and well-maintained landscaping. Old-fashioned cars sit parked out front. Everything looks … real.

"There you are!" The nurse is back, and she looks angry. "This is completely against the rules!"

You try to dodge her, but more nurses rush in to help.

"No!" You struggle to free yourself as they grab hold, but escape looks more unlikely with each new nurse who appears.

The Adirondack Cottage Sanatorium was built by
Dr. Edward Trudeau. He also founded a laboratory
and the Trudeau School of Tuberculosis.

"I'm not supposed to be here!" you yell, in one
final attempt for freedom. "I'm from the future!
And I'm not sick, I don't have tuberculosis,
please, you have to let me go ..."

In the end, though, there's no way you can
overpower six nurses. They wrestle you into a
straitjacket and lead you back inside.

Turn the page.

"Maybe this one ought to go to the asylum instead," one of them grumbles, rubbing a sore spot on her arm.

"Don't worry," your nurse says. "There will be plenty of time for personal reflection when we're back inside the sanatorium."

She turns to you and grins. "Plenty of time."

THE END

To follow another path, turn to page 10.
To learn more about tuberculosis and sanatoriums,
turn to page 99.

You've already run into one spirit in this spooky place. To encounter another one—and in this creepy basement—is more than you can take tonight. With a deep breath, you run through Ruth and charge back up the steps. A deathly chill passes through your bones. The farther you get from the ghost the warmer you feel.

Back out onto the first floor, you waste no time. Within minutes, you're through a window and outside into the cool night air. The sun has just set. Only a faint glow of orange remains in the sky.

"I didn't even make it to true nightfall," you mutter to yourself, feeling a little embarrassed to be giving up so quickly.

Then again, you reflect, you've seen more than enough tonight.

Turn the page.

You walk briskly down the gravel road, looking back over your shoulder at the hulking sanatorium. Your eyes are drawn to the third floor. You can't be sure, but you think you can make out a figure standing in one of the windows, looking out at you. Standing there, alone in that huge building, the figure looks very small and alone. You feel a wave of sadness.

No time for that, you tell yourself. You take another step forward, then another. You don't look back again.

THE END

To follow another path, turn to page 10.
To learn more about tuberculosis and sanatoriums,
turn to page 99.

The body chute gives you the creeps. But the thought of Ruth's ghost—or whatever that thing is—is far worse. With a deep breath, you charge in through the opening.

It's like stepping into a dungeon. An instant wave of claustrophobia overwhelms you. You feel like you can't breathe, like the walls are closing in all around you.

A glance over your shoulder is all you need to keep you going, though. A pale blue glow lights the room behind you. Whispers, just below the threshold of what you can make out, make the hairs on the back of your neck stand up.

Down the tunnel you go. It's lined with railroad tracks. You shiver, realizing that those were the tracks they used to wheel the dead bodies out of the hospital. How much death has this tunnel seen?

Turn the page.

Your footsteps echo off the walls as you hurry down, checking over your shoulder every few seconds, dreading the time when you'll see a pale blue glow lighting the tunnel walls.

Finally, after what seems an eternity, you feel a warm draft rising up from below. You break out into a sprint until you emerge outside onto a rocky landing. Loose stones and trash litter the ground. The sky above you is lit by moonlight.

Around 1.2 miles (2 kilometers) of tunnels can be found beneath Tranquille Sanatorium in British Columbia.

Part of you wants to stick around to investigate. But you can still imagine a faint blue glow coming down the chute behind you. No chance. It's time to get out of here and find your way home. You won't be coming back.

THE END

To follow another path, turn to page 10.
To learn more about tuberculosis and sanatoriums,
turn to page 99.

Everyone should get a last wish, you think. "I'll help you," you say grandly. But now that you've promised … how will you follow through? First, you have to get out of this room. Surprisingly, the door is unlocked.

"It's not a prison," the girl points out. "We're just not supposed to be wandering around."

The sanatorium in Beelitz had 60 buildings and operated as its own small village.

You sneak out and head up the stairs. Luckily they're next to the elevator, so you don't run into any other patients. The trip up the stairs is slow—you're still on the third floor, and there are still two stories to go. You have to stop often to let the sick children rest and catch their breath.

As you take another break just above the fourth floor, the stairwell door opens and a nurse steps though.

"Patients out of their rooms!" she yells. Another nurse rushes in to help.

"Go!" one of the boys tells you. He thrusts his open palm at you, and you feel a supernatural wave of energy push you. As you and the two other ghosts run, the boy collapses, drawing in pained breaths and letting out hacking coughs. The nurses stop to treat him, giving you the time you need to make it to the roof.

Turn the page.

You push the door open and the sun's warm rays bathe you in a comforting light. The two ghost children cry out in happiness. As you watch, they seem to dissolve. The last thing you see is the girl's smiling face. "Thank you," she whispers, a silver tear glinting in the corner of her eye.

When the ghosts finally disappear, the sunlight fades and day turns to night. The building returns to its graffitied, crumbling shell, leaving you alone on top of the haunted abandoned sanatorium.

THE END

To follow another path, turn to page 10.
To learn more about tuberculosis and sanatoriums,
turn to page 99.

No, you think. *I'm not going to give up. Not here!*

You begin to thrash around again. The water splashes, getting in your eyes, ears, nose, and mouth. But you keep moving, kicking and punching at the tub's fabric cover. You're blinded by saltwater, but your friends' voices seem to be getting louder, so you don't stop. Finally your fingers seem to catch a small tear in the fabric, and in one mighty motion you rip through.

Some sanatoriums hid the number of patient deaths by listing them as "discharged" instead of "deceased."

Turn the page.

Cold air rushes into your lungs as you burst out of the tub. Mitch catches you and Luisa helps you out.

Your clothes are dry, and your friends never heard any water running. But you know what you heard and felt. You dash to the building's entrance without a second glance and leave without even grabbing your stuff. Your haunted sanatorium adventure is over.

THE END

To follow another path, turn to page 10.
To learn more about tuberculosis and sanatoriums,
turn to page 99.

The warm water is soothing. Your friends' panicked voices seem further and further away as you tune them out. Soon you're lulled into a dreamless slumber.

Eventually, your friends, unable to move the tub's cover, leave to find help. But when they return hours later, there's no sign of your body. No one sees or hears from you ever again. The only clue left behind is a thin layer of moisture at the bottom of the tub.

THE END

To follow another path, turn to page 10.
To learn more about tuberculosis and sanatoriums,
turn to page 99.

Your first instinct is to get your friend out of here, as far from whatever that is as you can. Without even thinking about the danger, you dart into the room, hoping Mitch is right behind you.

He is. Together, you grab Luisa by the arms and drag her limp body out of the room. As you dive out through the doorway, the pale blue light flickers and brightens. A high-pitched, piercing scream fills the room, spilling out into the corridor beyond. The blue spirit surges toward the doorway, but it stops at the threshold. It's trapped inside the room, bound by some invisible force.

The face has changed. It no longer looks like a nurse. It's grown longer, with sharp angles. The eyes glow bright blue, and a narrow mouth is locked in a grimace.

What's left of the old door slams violently shut. You see the ghost's face through the holes in the door for only for a second—probably less—before it fades away. But the image, you know, will be burned into your mind forever.

By the time you look away from the closed door, Luisa is already regaining consciousness. "What did you see?" Mitch asks her. Her eyes show pure terror.

"No time to talk," you say, helping Luisa to her feet. "We're getting out of here, now."

Nobody argues. All three of you have come to the same realization. Trying to spend the night in a haunted sanatorium was not the best idea. You should be grateful you managed to get out with your sanity—and your life.

THE END

To follow another path, turn to page 10.
To learn more about tuberculosis and sanatoriums,
turn to page 99.

In that instant, your fear disappears. All you feel is anger and rage. Whatever that thing is, it's hurting your friend. With a roar, you charge at the ghost, diving over Luisa's unconscious body. You brace yourself for impact, but … nothing happens. You reach out for the ghost, but you pass right through. All you feel is a strange tingling sensation.

San Haven Sanatorium began as a tuberculosis clinic. Later it also accepted mentally handicapped patients.

You scramble to your feet. Your attack has gotten the ghost's attention. It no longer hangs over Luisa. Instead, it rises up, turning toward you. "Get her out," you shout to Mitch.

The spirit hovers closer … closer. Then it surges toward you. You try to dodge it, but it's impossible. The misty figure seems to grow with every passing second. It looms over you.

You try to shout for your friends. But a second later, the entire room begins to shake. At first, it's a tremor. But it grows stronger and stronger. Chunks of wall and ceiling break loose, raining down on you. A piece the size of a softball slams down on top of your head.

Your knees buckle, sending you sprawling to the ground. The shaking grows more and more violent. You cover your head with your arms as pieces of the ceiling crumble and fall.

Turn the page.

The old structure can't take the stress. A loud crack envelops the room, just seconds before the entire ceiling comes down.

You can only hope Mitch and Luisa got out before it was too late.

THE END

To follow another path, turn to page 10.
To learn more about tuberculosis and sanatoriums,
turn to page 99.

Stories seem a lot safer than looking for real ghosts. "Let's stay here," you say meekly. "I know, I've got a story about a headless vampire."

Luisa shrugs, and you can see a look of relief on Mitch's face. You tell your story of the headless vampire, which ends up being not very scary at all. Even so, you all have a great time laughing and joking.

And so it goes for the rest of the night. A bump in the night here. A strange squeak or unexplained cold draft there. You shrug it off, telling yourself that it's nothing but your imagination.

You don't ever even bother leaving the main entrance. In time, the stories die out, the laughing stops, and you all drift off to sleep.

Turn the page.

Your dreams are troubled. You can't quite remember the details come morning, but the image of three sick children playing in the hospital's hallways lingers with you. It leaves you with a lingering sense of loneliness that you can't quite shake.

"Let's get out of here," Mitch says as you all stretch your sore muscles. Before you leave, you look back into the building, suddenly regretful that you left it unexplored. *What was the point of coming here*, you ask yourself, *if we weren't even going to look around a little?*

Maybe you'll get another chance someday. If you do, you vow to take it.

THE END

To follow another path, turn to page 10.
To learn more about tuberculosis and sanatoriums, turn to page 99.

"That way!" you shout, pointing to the fire escape. It's closer than the stairwell, and you want to get out of here as quickly as you can. As you sprint down the hallway, you can feel the shadow looming behind you, watching you … hunting you. Your mind races. What if the door is locked? You'll be trapped.

Panicked, you throw yourself into the fire escape door. To your relief, it opens. The three of you spill out into the night. Quickly you whirl and lean in to close the door. For an instant, you see it—the shadow, ready to envelop everything in front of it. Then the door clicks shut.

Your heart races. You're drenched in sweat. For a few seconds, you stand, frozen to the spot, staring at the door, half expecting it to fly open, with a shadow bursting out toward you.

Turn the page.

That doesn't happen. Seconds pass. Minutes. All is quiet.

Finally, Mitch breaks the spell by speaking. "Come on. Let's get out of here. The stairs lead down to the ground."

"Should we go back to get our stuff first?" Luisa asks.

You and Mitch answer in unison. "NO!"

You'll come back tomorrow, during daylight, to get what you left behind.

On second thought, you might not even do that.

Then you grin. Maybe you can get Ethan to get it instead.

THE END

To follow another path, turn to page 10.
To learn more about tuberculosis and sanatoriums,
turn to page 99.

You look toward the fire escape. It's closer, but you have no idea whether the door is locked or not. "Go back! Go back!" you shout, turning back toward the stairwell and sprinting down the hallway.

Luisa is in front of you, with Mitch staying close. All three of you dash down the hallway as fast as you can. You can feel the darkness behind you, growing larger, faster, closing in on you. The walls themselves crack and creak as the shadow scrambles across them.

The stairwell is 30 feet away … then 20. *Almost there* … you think, when a frigid blast of cold shakes your body. Your legs freeze, and you trip. "Go! Go!" Mitch shouts, pulling you to your feet and propelling you forward.

Turn the page.

You're just a few strides from the stairwell when Luisa stumbles too. She goes down in a heap, and you're following so closely that you never have a chance. You tumble head-first over her, and then Mitch over you.

Luisa screams. The shadow is descending upon you. Desperately, you try shining your flashlight onto it. But the darkness seems to just swallow up the light.

The last thing you ever see is the eyes. They're like pools of the deepest darkness, swirling and stirring. They're not of this world, that much is certain. Within moments, you won't be either.

THE END

To follow another path, turn to page 10.
To learn more about tuberculosis and sanatoriums,
turn to page 99.

The nurse looks down at you, waiting for an answer. Your mind races, your heart pounds, and every shallow breath is a challenge. You need help. You need something. Desperate for relief, you nod your head.

"Very well," says the nurse. She helps you lie back. "Here we go."

You close your eyes, trying to relax.

patients at a sanatorium in the Czech Republic, circa 1940

Turn the page.

You expect to feel something small, like a prick of static electricity. Instead the electrical current that jolts into you causes every muscle in your body to seize. The violent shock of it causes you to bolt upright, screaming.

As the echoes of your scream die away, you look around you. The nurse is gone; so is the strange haze. The walls are chipped and cracked again. Two young faces stare at you, jaws dropped. It takes a moment for you to realize that you're back. Your hands are shaking, and you're drenched in sweat, but you're back.

You try to explain it to Mitch and Luisa. But they both look at you like you're crazy. They're very kind and very gentle as they lead you out of the hospital. "Let's get you home," Mitch says. You don't argue.

You can never explain what happened to you on that table. No one would understand. You don't even understand. As the days and weeks pass, you become convinced it was some strange waking dream. Yet sometimes you still wake up at night in a cold sweat, grasping at your throat and gasping for air.

THE END

To follow another path, turn to page 10.
To learn more about tuberculosis and sanatoriums,
turn to page 99.

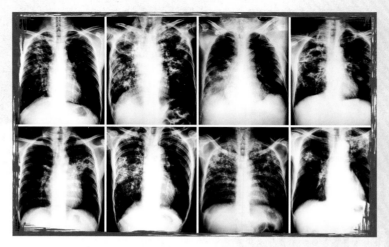

Tuberculosis commonly attacks the lungs. However, other parts of the body can be affected too. The weight loss caused by tuberculosis seemed to consume the sick—which is why the disease is sometimes known as consumption.

Therapy? Something about the way the nurse says the word sends a chill down your spine. You violently shake your head no, but the movement sends you into a horrible and painful fit of coughing.

The nurse wheels you back to your room. As you enter, you notice the room's window stands wide open, despite the cold night air.

You point to the window, knowing that it should be closed. But the nurse just shakes her head. "Now, now, you know that fresh air is the best cure," she scolds as she covers you up.

"We'll try again with the shock treatment in the morning," she says, gently patting your shoulder. But you can tell by the look on her face that she really doesn't expect you to make it through the night.

The night wears on. The cold night air chills your lungs. The pressure in your chest and throat becomes crushing. The lack of oxygen to your brain leaves you constantly confused and unable to think clearly. What is this place? You can't shake the feeling that you don't belong. But your memory is a blank, and the fits of coughing and pain make it impossible to really search your confused thoughts and memories.

Turn the page.

You sleep, racked by all-too-familiar dreams of another time, of faces you know, whose names you cannot remember. You seem caught between worlds, trapped, unable to escape.

But your body is growing weaker by the hour. You won't be trapped long. The end is near.

THE END

To follow another path, turn to page 10.
To learn more about tuberculosis and sanatoriums,
turn to page 99.

"Let's just keep going," you suggest. "Luisa, you wanted to see the morgue. Let's do that."

She shrugs her shoulders. "Sure thing."

The three of you creep down the hallway until you spot the door marked MORGUE. It's open. The three of you slip inside. It's pitch black, aside from the three beams of your flashlights.

"Whoa," Mitch says. "It's creepy in here."

He's right. A light, the bulbs long since burned out, hangs over a rusted steel bed. Open doors cut into the wall reveal body-sized cubbies. One still has a rack installed to slide bodies in and out, but none of you are brave enough to jump on yourselves.

Suddenly the room seems to grow colder. Shivering, you wrap your arms around yourself.

Turn the page.

That's when you hear the footsteps. All three of you freeze in place. You watch as a figure—pale, white, and transparent—strolls past the open doorway. So slender it appears almost skeletal, the mysterious figure appears to be wearing a hospital gown.

Seconds pass. "Wh-what did we just see?" Mitch stammers. But you all have a pretty good idea already.

You gather your courage and stick your head out the door. You're almost disappointed to find that the corridor is empty. No one is here.

You take a cautious step outside, and then stand, listening. Without any notice, the sound of footsteps returns. Before you even have time to duck back inside, the figure—the ghost—materializes out of thin air.

It's an old man, bald and gaunt. His eyes are deep pockets of pure black. Yet, as your heart races and fear wells up inside your chest, he doesn't seem threatening. For a long moment, he just stares at you.

Finally, the ghost speaks. You can make out the words, but they sound more like a rattle than a voice. "You don't belong here," he says. You can't take your eyes off those hollow pits of black. "They won't let you stay."

Some people believe that morgues are always haunted.

Turn the page.

With that, the ghost shuffles off down the hallway. As you watch him go, his figure slowly fades away into nothingness. It's as if he never existed at all.

But all three of you saw him. And all three heard him. "That wasn't a threat," you tell your friends. "That was a warning."

Luisa scoffs. "Yeah, super scary," she says, rolling her eyes.

Suddenly, the entire building shakes. A chilling, ghostly voice echoes through the hallway. "LEAVE NOW!" it screams.

"Consider me warned," Mitch says. "Let's get out of here!"

THE END

To follow another path, turn to page 10.
To learn more about tuberculosis and sanatoriums,
turn to page 99.

You fear for your friend, but you also fear for yourself. In an action that will haunt you the rest of your life, you back away. You trip over the debris left behind from the door, and crawl out of the room on all fours.

"Where are you going!?" Mitch yells. "We have to help her!"

"Y-y-you ... you help Luisa!" you stammer. "I ... I'll go for help! I'll be back, I promise!"

"Don't you dare leave!" Mitch screams. "Don't you dare!"

His back is turned to the ghost, so he doesn't see as the nurse rises in the air behind him. Mist rolls off her body, and the blue light coming from her seems to intensify. She spreads her arms and reaches toward your friend.

Turn the page.

You don't wait to see what happens next. Half-stumbling, you use the walls to help propel you back toward the main entrance. You hear screaming—is it Mitch, or is it you? Maybe it's both. You cover your ears to block it out.

You find your way to the front door and propel yourself out. The moment your foot hits the grass, you fall to your knees, gasping for breath.

The ground rumbles. You feel the building shake behind you. You turn over and watch as the walls slowly begin to crumble. Windows are crushed, spraying bits of glass everywhere. Then the entire sanatorium collapses, leaving a huge cloud of dust in the air.

"MITCH!" you scream. "LUISA!" You call their names over and over. But nobody answers.

You're hoarse by the time the fire department arrives. They call an ambulance, but the emergency workers can't find anything wrong with you. Police officers ask you question after question, but you don't know how to answer any of them.

No signs of your friends are found in the wreckage. Their families are devastated. There's nothing you can do to help them, because nobody believes the truth.

When you close your eyes at night, ghostly nurses and the faces of your missing friends haunt your dreams.

THE END

To follow another path, turn to page 10.
To learn more about tuberculosis and sanatoriums,
turn to page 99.

EPILOGUE: THE WHITE PLAGUE

Spread from person to person, tuberculosis bacteria attacks a person's lungs, and can cause—among other things—chest pain, coughing, fever and chills, loss of appetite, and fatigue. This contagious disease is easily spread through sneezing, coughing, and talking. One person can infect 10 to 15 other people in a year.

The bacteria can also enter a person's body and lie dormant. Then years, or even decades, later, the bacteria can attack.

Tuberculosis, also known as consumption, TB, and the White Plague, was a common disease in the 1700s to early 1900s. However, even today it is still the leading cause of death worldwide. Every year millions of people contract the disease.

Sanatoriums are medical facilities to treat patients with long-term illnesses—most commonly tuberculosis. The first sanatorium in America was built in 1885. They were meant to provide patients with a clean, sanitary environment surrounded only by health care workers and patients who were already infected. Ideal tuberculosis facilities included fresh air, good nutrition, and good health care.

By 1900 tuberculosis was the second-most common cause of death in the United States. As concern over public health began to improve, sanatoriums became more common. In 1900 there were 34 sanatoriums across the country, with fewer than 5,000 beds. By 1925, 536 sanatoriums had been built and more than 670,000 beds were available. By the 1940s around 1,000 sanatoriums had opened.

Today many of those sanatoriums lie empty. The number of people who died behind their doors is just one reason people believe that at least a few of them are haunted.

RULES AND ROUTINES

Detailed routines dominated patients' daily lives. They were encouraged to stay idle to avoid irritating their infected lungs. Movement was minimized, and even simple tasks such as reading or knitting were discouraged.

Sanatorium rules were strict and expected to be followed. Patients were instructed to never run, walk fast, or do anything that might physically tire them (or even cause them to be out of breath). There were also rules on how to cough, and what could and could not be discussed between patients—including a person's health and likelihood of getting better.

Many patients found their schedules boring and oppressive. A lot of time spent doing nothing, along with being separated from friends and family, was hard on sanatorium patients. Some people think their ghosts may feel that separation in death too. Some sanatorium ghosts are said to be lonely spirits that are just waiting for someone to talk and to play with them.

TREATMENTS

Both hydrotherapy and electroshock therapy were common treatments for tuberculosis.

Continuous baths as a form of hydrotherapy were meant to calm the mind. Patients were left in a tub for several hours or even overnight. The tub water temperature would be closely regulated. Canvas covers would help maintain the water's temperature. When done correctly, this could be a relaxing session.

However, it could also be abused. When filled with ice water, baths were used to tire restless patients. The baths were also useful for restraining patients for extended periods of time.

Electroshock therapy started in the 1930s. Small electric currents to the brain can stimulate the brain in different ways. It is still used today to treat some mental illnesses. But, like any treatment, it can be (and was) overused.

Shocks could be given to overactive or depressed patients. Often they would wake tired or confused. The treatment could also put a disruptive patient to sleep. Sometimes people who received electroshock treatments never mentally recovered. Today ghost hunters seek out those spirits that may linger, still angry about the injustices they faced in life.

TUBERCULOSIS TODAY

A vaccine against tuberculosis was developed in the early 1920s, and the first effective antibiotic was developed in 1944. These vastly decreased the disease's spread in North America and Europe. With fewer patients to treat, many sanatoriums closed their doors forever.

However, tuberculosis remains the leading cause of death among young adults around the world. About 9 million people contract the disease every year, and more than 1.5 million die.

Most cases of tuberculosis are curable with proper treatment. There are 10 drugs approved by the U.S. Food and Drug Administration for treating tuberculosis, and patients usually take a combination of at least several drugs for six months to as long as a year.

However, proper treatment is key, and not everyone has access to medical care or the right antibiotics. If treatment is stopped early, the patient will still be contagious. And, in some cases, the bacteria is resistant to one or more anti-tuberculosis drugs. In the 1990s there was an outbreak of multidrug-resistant tuberculosis in New York City that cost nearly $1 billion to control.

Tuberculosis has, and will continue to be, a problem we struggle to cure. There are dozens of famous sanatoriums across the country to prove this point. Today some of those buildings are completely abandoned. Others operate as museums, or as places of study for paranormal researchers. Curious visitors may be able to take haunted tours or guided visits. Would you be brave enough to visit at one of them?

TIMELINE

1882—Robert Koch isolates the bacteria that causes tuberculosis. He receives a Nobel Prize in 1905.

1884—Edward Livingston Trudeau opens the first American sanatorium, Adirondack Cottage, in Saranac Lake, New York.

1890—Dr. Charles Mantoux creates the Mantoux tuberculin skin test, which determines whether a person is infected with tuberculosis.

1898—Beelitz-Heilstätten is built in Beelitz, Germany; it is Germany's largest sanatorium.

1904—The National Tuberculosis Association (now known as the American Lung Association) is founded.

1905—35 acres (14 hectares) are set aside for the Pokegama Sanatorium in Pine City, Minnesota.

1907—Tranquille Sanatorium (also known as Serenity Lake Sanatorium) in Kamloops, British Columbia, Canada, opens. Legend says that it is mysteriously abandoned in 1958, with no sign of staff anywhere.

September 7, 1907—The Michigan State Sanatorium opens in Howell, Michigan.

1908—French scientists Albert Calmette and Camille Guérin are able to grow the tuberculosis bacteria in a lab. The first tuberculosis vaccine, Bacillus Calmette-Guérin (BCG), is introduced in 1921.

July 23, 1910—Waverly Hills Sanatorium opens in Louisville, Kentucky.

1912—San Haven Sanatorium opens near Dunseith, North Dakota. It later becomes a mental hospital in the late 1950s.

July 15, 1916—The first patients are brought to St. Albans Sanatorium in Radford, Virginia.

1916—Adolf Hitler is sent to Beelitz-Heilstätten, now a military hospital, to recover from war wounds. (Some people today call it Hitler's Hospital.)

1938—Electrotherapy is first developed.

1944—Antibiotics are first used against tuberculosis.

1985—Tuberculosis cases in the United States begin to rise. Crowded housing, immigration from countries where tuberculosis is common, lack of proper treatment, and a rise in HIV/AIDS are a few possible causes.

mid–1980s–early 1990s—A strain of multidrug-resistant tuberculosis spreads through New York City.

1993—The World Health Organization declares tuberculosis a worldwide epidemic.

2014—The World Health Assembly approves a plan, called the End TB Strategy, with the goal to completely wipe out tuberculosis by 2034.

GLOSSARY

antibiotic (an-ti-bye-OT-ik)—a drug that kills bacteria and is used to cure infections and disease

asylum (uh-SY-luhm)—hospital for people who are mentally ill

bacteria (bak-TEER-ee-uh)—one-celled, tiny living things; some are helpful and some cause disease

claustrophobia (KLAH-struh-foe-bee-uh)—the fear of tight spaces

contagious (kun-TAY-juss)—spreadable, as in disease

debris (duh-BREE)—the scattered pieces of something that has been broken or destroyed

dormant (DOR-muhnt)—not active

graffiti (gruh-FEE-tee)—pictures drawn or words written with spray paint on buildings, bridges, and trains; most graffiti is illegal.

hydrotherapy (HYE-druh-THER-uh-pee)—treating a medical condition with hot baths and/or steam

instinct (IN-stingkt)—behavior that is natural rather than learned

isolation (eye-suh-LAY-shun)—the condition of being alone

morgue (MORG)—a place where dead bodies are kept until they are identified or released for burial oppressive (o-PRES-ihv)—the treatment of people in a cruel, unjust, and hard way

sanatorium (san-uh-TOR-i-uhm)—a place for the care and treatment of people recovering from illness

static electricity (STAH-tik i-lek-TRISS-uh-tee)—the buildup of an electrical charge on the surface of an object

supernatural (soo-pur-NACH-ur-uhl)—something that cannot be given an ordinary explanation

tuberculosis (tu-BUR-kyoo-low-sis)—a disease caused by bacteria that causes fever, weight loss, and coughing; left untreated, tuberculosis can lead to death.

urban legend (UR-buhn LEJ-uhnd)—a story about an event or piece of information told as though it were true

vaccine (VAK-seen)—a medicine that prevents a disease

vandalize (VAN-duhl-ize)—to needlessly damage property

OTHER PATHS TO EXPLORE

In this book you've seen how terrifying being alone in a haunted place can be. But haunted places can mean different things to different people. Seeing an experience from many points of view is an important part of understanding it.

Here are a few ideas for other haunted points of view to explore:

- Imagine you are a patient in a sanatorium. What would you do to pass the time? Who would you miss the most? What would you bring along?

- Hydrotherapy and electroshock therapy could be part of a patient's daily routine. Which would you rather experience?

- Sanatoriums were full of sick people. They couldn't operate without doctors, nurses, and other support staff. What might it have been like to work in a sanatorium?

READ MORE

Chandler, Matt. *Alcatraz: A Chilling Interactive Adventure.* North Mankato, Minn.: Capstone Press, 2017.

Davis, Jamie. *Haunted Asylums, Prisons, and Sanatoriums: Inside the Abandoned Institutions for the Crazy, Criminal, & Quarantined.* Woodbury, Minn.: Llewellyn Publications, 2013.

Morey, Allan. *12 Spooky Haunted Places.* Mankato, Minn.: 12-Story Library, 2016.

INTERNET SITES

Use FactHound to find Internet sites related to this book. All of the sites on FactHound have been researched by our staff.

Here's all you do:
Visit *www.facthound.com*
Type in this code: 9781515736516

INDEX